Little Baby
Steps™
to
Success

STARBURST  PUBLISHERS™

P.O. Box 4123, Lancaster, Pennsylvania 17604

Credits:
To schedule Author appearances write:
Author Appearances, Starburst Promotions, P.O. Box 4123
Lancaster, Pennsylvania 17604 or call (717) 293-0939.

Cover art by David Marty Design.
Scripture Quotations are from The Holy Bible:
King James Version; New International Version—Copyright 1984 by The International Bible Society and
published by Zondervan Bible Publishers.

"Little" Baby Steps to Success

First Printing, September 1997

ISBN: 0-914984-969
Library of Congress Catalog Number 96-072371

Printed in the United States of America.

More Baby Steps!

Baby Steps to Success: *52 Vince Lombardi-Inspired Ways to Make Your Life Successful.* Vince Lombardi's is one of the most quoted success stories in the history of the world. The same skills that Coach Lombardi used to turn the Green Bay Packers from cellar dwellers to world champions is now available in 52 unique and achievable "baby steps."

Baby Steps to Happiness: *52 Inspiring Ways to Make Your Life Happy.* This unique 52-step approach will enable the reader to focus on small steps that bring practical and proven change. Chapter titles, such as, *Have a Reason to Get Out of Bed, Deal with Your Feelings or Become Them, Would You Rather Be Right or Happy?* and *Love To Win More Than You Hate to Lose* give insight and encouragement on the road to happiness.

Little Baby Steps to Happiness: *Inspiring Quotes and Affirmations to Make Your Life Happy.* This portable collection of quotes and affirmations from *Baby Steps to Happiness* will encourage happiness one little footstep at a time.

See pages 159—160 for more information

Acknowledgments

The authors wish to thank: Terry Bledsoe for his tremendous help and input. Thanks to Jill Lombardi for her love and patience. Also, the same to Vincent, John, Gina, and Joe. Likewise thanks to Harrison Baucom for multiple hours of typing, research, editing, and finding quotes; Carol Rogers for obsessive and compulsive editing; Keppy Baucom for research and quotes; Shannon McKnight for organizing, editing, inspiring, and otherwise supervising; Butch Simpson, Barry Wagner, Ken Martin, Sam Dinacola, and Elaine Perryman for their input; Clairalyn, Jeremy, Benjamin, Valerie, Chip, and Sheri for their help and inspiration.

Dedication

To the memory of Coach Vincent Lombardi and all those who follow his dream.

Success can be yours. It begins this moment. Take a baby step by moving toward a worthwhile goal. Success is in the journey as well as the destination.

The spirit, the will to win, and the will to excel—these are the things that endure and these are the qualities that are so much more important than any of the events that occasion them.

—Coach Lombardi

Success is action and doing. You must act on the right ideas. The ideas are here. Only you can act. Do it now.

There comes a moment when you have to stop revving up the car and shove it into gear.

—David Mahoney

True success is a way of life. It's not a short-term achievement and then burning out. Real success is a lifestyle, one baby step at a time.

The good Lord gave you a body that can stand most anything. It's your mind you have to convince.
—Coach Lombardi

To achieve, you must believe. Believe in your goal. But more importantly believe in yourself. Success is certain only if you believe in yourself.

Act as if it were impossible to fail.

—Dorothea Brande

Change your belief and you will change your life. The quality of your beliefs will determine the quality of your life.

In any project the important factor is your belief. Without belief there can be no successful outcome.
—William James

Little Baby Steps to Success

Your level of success is not determined by your work. Thousands of workaholics die annually from lack of belief. Without strong self-belief no success is possible.

Success is a habit. Winning is a habit. Unfortunately so is losing.

—Coach Lombardi

Vision is like a compass. It points the way. Without a clear vision you can be lost. Make your vision worthwhile. Then your direction will be the same.

A man can be as great as he wants to be.
—Coach Lombardi

Vision is not a dream. It's a future reality, yet to be brought into existence. What do you want for your future? That's your vision.

Where there is no vision, the people perish.
—Proverbs 29:18a

Don't limit your vision by what's possible today. Make it inspiring and almost out of reach. Remember it's your future reality.

You see things; and you say, "Why?" But I dream things that never were; and I say, "Why not?"
—George Bernard Shaw

Self-talk happens constantly, whether or not you're aware of it. Take charge of your self-talk and eliminate self-criticism.

If we will create something, we must be something. Character is the direct result of mental attitude.

—Coach Lombardi

In the absence of a chosen positive thought, your mind reverts to negativity. Make a positive choice. Then follow it with positive self-talk.

As long as you're going to think anyway, think big.
—Donald Trump

Even highly successful people are occasionally self-critical. When you do the same, replace each criticism with affirmations. This will ease your journey to success.

Teams do not go physically flat, they go mentally stale.

—Coach Lombardi

Little Baby Steps to Success

Examine your life relentlessly. Make adjustments when necessary. It takes courage. But successful people will tell you it's what made the difference in their achievement.

Not failure, but low aim, is crime.

—James Russell Lowell

If "the unexamined life is not worth living," then make your life worthwhile. Examine it with fervor. Only then will you know what changes to make.

Examine yourselves, whether ye be in the faith.
—2 Corinthians 13:5a

This is your life. You're responsible for it. If you're unsatisfied, conduct a thorough examination of the unhealthy choices you've made. Then make new ones.

Coach Lombardi showed me that by working hard and using my mind, I could overcome my weakness to the point where I could be one of the best.

—Bart Starr,
Hall of Fame Quarterback, Green Bay Packers

Find meaning in your life. If it's not there, create it. Meaning does not have to be in your job. But it does have to be in your life.

Unless you try to do something beyond what you have already mastered, you will never grow.

—Ronald E. Osborn

Dr. Viktor Frankl said meaning gives substance to life. He described it as the most significant factor separating successful people from those who quit. He was right.

Unless a man believes in himself and makes a total commitment to his career and puts everything he has into it—his mind, his body, and his life—what is life worth to him?

—Coach Lombardi

Build meaning into your daily life. Make this commitment. If it's meaningless, don't do it. You will be far more successful.

Lord, grant that I may always desire more than I can accomplish.

—Michelangelo

Little Baby Steps to Success

Inner direction is listening to the beat of your own drummer. Listen closely. It's the drumming of your heart. Follow the rhythm. You will be successful.

If you're lucky enough to find a guy with a lot of head and heart, he's never going to come off the field second.

—Coach Lombardi

Others will tell you it can't be done. Smile. But don't march to the beat of their drum. Continue working toward your goal. You will succeed.

The world is moving so fast these days that the man who says it can't be done is generally interrupted by someone doing it.

—Harry Emerson Fosdick

Being inner directed will not necessarily make you popular. But it will make you successful.

I demand a commitment to excellence and to victory and that is what life is all about.

—Coach Lombardi

Some people dream. Others succeed. The difference is often self-discipline.

No one should negotiate their dreams. Dreams must be free to flee and fly high. No government, no legislature, has a right to limit your dreams. You should never agree to surrender your dreams.
—Reverend Jesse Jackson

Self-discipline is the capacity to do what you *need* to do, rather than what you *want* to do. It's difficult, but the result is worth it.

Leaders are made, they are not born. They are made by hard effort, which is the price which all of us must pay to achieve any goal that is worthwhile.
—Coach Lombardi

Little Baby Steps to Success

Systematically plan and carry out your vision, mission, and goals. You will then be self-disciplined. Success is the inevitable result.

He that hath no rule over his own spirit is like a city that is broken down, and without walls.

—Proverbs 25:28

You have priorities, though you may not think in those terms. Investigate what's really important. It will help you on the road to success.

Only three things should matter to you: your religion, your family and the Green Bay Packers. In that order.
—Coach Lombardi

Most people spend their lives *reacting* to urgencies. Be different. *Act on* priorities. You will be one of the few who are truly successful.

Put your heart, mind, intellect, and soul even to your smallest acts. This is the secret of success.
—Sivananda Sarasvati

Make a list of your priorities. Act on the important things daily. The urgent ones will take care of themselves.

Once you have established the goals you want and the price you're willing to pay, you can ignore the minor hurts, the opponent's pressure and temporary failures.

—Coach Lombardi

Little Baby Steps to Success

We all have the same amount of time. It's what you do with it that makes the difference. Use this moment wisely. It's your only chance.

I believe a man should be on time, not a minute late, not ten seconds late . . . I believe that a man who's late for meetings or for the bus won't run his pass routes right. He'll be sloppy.

—Coach Lombardi

Little Baby Steps to Success

Carpe Diem. Seize the day. *Carpe momentum*. Seize the moment. Do it. And you're well on the road to success.

To every thing there is a season, and a time to every purpose under heaven.

—Ecclesiastes 3:1

Often the best medicine for what ails you is this. Do something meaningful in the time you have available. Do it now.

Just don't give up trying to do what you really want to do . . . . Where there's love and inspiration, I don't think you can go wrong.

—Ella Fitzgerald

A successful life is composed of successful goals. A second goal begins when you've achieved the first. It's a perpetual journey.

Heroes are made in the hour of defeat. Success is, therefore, well described as a series of glorious defeats.

—Mohandas K. Gandhi

Successful people have goals. They also enjoy the journey of working on them, as much as achieving them.

Once a man has made a commitment to a way of life, he puts the greatest strength in the world behind him. It's something we call heart power. Once a man has made this commitment, nothing will stop him short of success.

—Coach Lombardi

Little Baby Steps to Success

You can't be successful without having high goals. Set them almost out of reach. Be inspired by your goals. And enjoy reaching them.

If we did all we are capable of doing we would literally astonish ourselves.

—Thomas Edison

Every successful business has a mission statement. So do successful people. Write a mission statement for your life. It will help you focus on success.

There is only one success—to be able to spend your life in your own way.

—Christopher Morley

You have priorities, though you may not think in those terms. Investigate what's really important. It will help you on the road to success.

Only three things should matter to you: your religion, your family and the Green Bay Packers. In that order.
—Coach Lombardi

Most people spend their lives *reacting* to urgencies. Be different. *Act on* priorities. You will be one of the few who are truly successful.

Put your heart, mind, intellect, and soul even to your smallest acts. This is the secret of success.
—Sivananda Sarasvati

Little Baby Steps to Success

Carpe Diem. **Seize the day.** *Carpe momentum.* **Seize the moment. Do it. And you're well on the road to success.**

To every thing there is a season, and a time to every purpose under heaven.

—Ecclesiastes 3:1

Often the best medicine for what ails you is this. Do something meaningful in the time you have available. Do it now.

Just don't give up trying to do what you really want to do . . . Where there's love and inspiration, I don't think you can go wrong.

—Ella Fitzgerald

Little Baby Steps to Success

Your mission statement is your blueprint for success. Success strategies are built on it. It may be only a few sentences long. But it's vital for success.

A man can be as great as he wants to be. If you believe in yourself and have the courage, the determination, the dedication, the competitive drive and if you are willing to sacrifice the little things in life and pay the price for the things that are worthwhile, it can be done.

—Coach Lombardi

Little Baby Steps to Success

Your "mission" is something to feel zealous about. Believe in it. Embrace it. Act on it. And you'll be well on the road to success.

Whatever your hand finds to do, do it with all your might.

—Ecclesiastes 9:10a NIV

Your vision and goals focus on a destination. Plans make up the map that help you reach the destination. Plan methodically for success.

Confidence comes from planning and practicing well. You get ready during the week and the confidence will be there on Sunday. This confidence is a difficult thing to explain. But you do get it if you have prepared.

—Coach Lombardi

Little Baby Steps to Success

Successful people plan far more than the average person. There's an explanation. It works! If you want to succeed, plan for success.

No one can arrive from being talented alone. God gives talent, work transforms talent into genius.
                                                    —Anna Pavlova

Japanese time management experts say you reap a 12 to 1 return ratio for time spent planning. German experts claim is 8 to 1. Either way, it pays to plan.

You might reduce Lombardi's coaching philosophy to a single sentence: In any game, you do the things you do best and you do them over and over and over.
—George Halas

Always have a contingency plan. It's like a spare tire. You hope not to use it. But it's there if necessary.

The will to succeed is important, but what's even more important is the will to prepare.

—Bobby Knight

Parachuting is a safe and exciting sport. But you still carry a reserve chute. Life is safe and exciting as well. But pack a "reserve" just in case. It's safer.

RULE OF SURVIVAL: Pack your own parachute.
—T.L. Hakala

Little Baby Steps to Success

There will be times when things just don't go right. Don't give up. Back up! Take another path. Maybe there's an alternate route. Take it.

You do what you can for as long as you can, and when you finally can't, you do the next best thing. You back up but you don't give up.

—Chuck Yeager

Focus is difficult. There is so much going on in your life. But focus is also necessary for success. Focus. Then focus again. You will succeed.

Success demands singleness of purpose.

—Coach Lombardi

". . . I do one thing. I do it well. Then I move on . . ." Charles Emerson Winchester III said it in the TV series *Mash.* Focus.

I don't know the key to success, but the key to failure is trying to please everybody.

—Bill Cosby

Little Baby Steps to Success

Success is like marksmanship. You won't hit the target unless you focus and aim. Focus. It's necessary for success.

The price of success is hard work, dedication to the job at hand and the determination that whether we win or lose, we have applied the best of ourselves to the task at hand.

—Coach Lombardi

Focus, but focus on the right thing. Sometimes you may need a reality check. Have friends who can provide that occasionally.

A leader must be honest with himself and know that as a leader he is just like everybody else.
—Coach Lombardi

Sometimes it's easy to stray. You think you're on the right path. Then you realize you took a wrong turn. It happens. Compensate and go on.

Then you will know the truth, and the truth will set you free.

—John 8:32 NIV

Life provides its own report card. It's called success. If you're not pleased with your grades, you've probably been studying for the wrong exam!

Fundamentals win it. Football is two things: it's blocking and it's tackling. I don't care anything about formation or new offenses or tricks on defense. If you block and tackle better than the team you're playing, you'll win.

—Coach Lombardi

Cortez burned his ships after invading Mexico. His soldiers had no choice but to fight and win. There was no turning back. That's commitment. Burn your ships.

If you want to be successful, it's just this simple: Know what you're doing. Love what you're doing. And believe in what you're doing.

—Will Rogers

Commitment is magic. Focus. Ensure you're focused on the right thing. And then commit to it. You will inevitably succeed.

If you fellows don't want to give me a hundred percent, get on up to the club house and turn in your equipment.

—Coach Lombardi

Comedians joke about men fearing commitment. It's not commitment they fear. It's failure. Don't be driven by fear. Commit and you will be driven by success.

Those who dare to fail miserably can achieve greatly.

—Robert F. Kennedy

Success requires struggle. It necessitates sacrifice. If you want to succeed, prepare for some suffering. But the price is worth it.

To achieve success we must pay a price for success. It's like anything worthwhile. You have to pay the price to win and you have to pay the price to get to the point where success is possible. Most important, you must pay the price to stay there.

—Coach Lombardi

Little Baby Steps to Success

Success is not purchased on credit, or the easy payment plan. It's earned by the sweat of your brow, one baby step at a time. Sacrifice is required.

Victory is not won in miles, but in inches. Win a little now, hold your ground, and later win a little more.
—Louis L'Amour

Little Baby Steps to Success

To reach any goal requires sacrifice. You'll have to give up something. You can have anything you want. But not everything you want. Sacrifice for success.

Do not love sleep or you will grow poor; stay awake and you will have food to spare.

—Proverbs 20:13 NIV

The journey to success is often arduous. It can only be negotiated if you're mentally tough. Condition your mind for success.

Mental toughness is many things and rather difficult to explain. Its qualities are sacrifice and self-denial. Also, most importantly, it is combined with a perfectly disciplined will that refuses to give in. It's a state of mind—you could call it character in action.

—Coach Lombardi

Failure is most often the result of giving up mentally. To succeed, convince yourself you deserve it. Then you're on the right path.

Always bear in mind that your own resolution to success is more important than any other one thing.
—Abraham Lincoln

All failure results from state of mind. So does all success. Mental toughness programs your "computer" mind to succeed.

Some of us will do our jobs well and some will not, but we will all be judged by only one thing—the result.
—Coach Lombardi

Little Baby Steps to Success

Work ethic is the willingness to put effort toward reaching a goal. To succeed requires an enormous amount of work. Enjoy it.

The harder you work, the harder it is to surrender.
—Coach Lombardi

Michelangelo said, "If they knew how hard I work, they wouldn't call it genius." Want to succeed? Work hard.

Opportunities are usually disguised by hard work, so most people don't recognize them.

—Ann Landers

Success? It's found in your effort and toil. Find a successful person. You'll find them standing beside a pool of sweat.

I never knew an early-rising hard-working, prudent man, careful of his earnings and strictly honest, who complained of hard luck. A good character, good habits and hard work are impregnable to the assaults of all ill-luck fools ever dreamed of.

—Joseph Addison

Your life's work may not be your job. It's your legacy. Sometimes they're the same thing. But it's rare. Build your life's work. It's holy.

Men for the sake of getting a living forget to live.
—Margaret Fuller

NFL commentator John Madden said he'd be doing the same thing even if he weren't getting paid for it. He loves what he does. It's his life work.

The secret to success is to do the common things uncommonly well.

—John D. Rockefeller, Jr.

If your life feels empty, it may be because you haven't discovered your life's work. Focus on it. It's a baby step on the road to success.

I don't think he (Coach Lombardi) ever taught me any football. What he'd do three times a week was preach on life.

—Henry Jordan,
Defensive Tackle, Green Bay Packers

You become good at what you practice. If you practice success skills, you become successful.

You teach discipline by doing it over and over, by repetition and rote, especially in a game like football when you have very little time to decide what you are going to do. So what you do is react almost instinctively, naturally. You have done it so many times, over and over again.

—Coach Lombardi

Practice. But be careful what you practice. If you practice failure, you will become good at it. If you practice success habits, you'll become good at them.

Do not neglect your gift, which was given you through a prophetic message when the body of elders laid their hands on you.

—1 Timothy 4:14 NIV

Begin developing success skills today. Practice one baby step daily. At the end of the year you will become a success.

Only those who have the patience to do simple things perfectly will acquire the skill to do difficult things easily.

—Johann Christoph von Schiller

To succeed at a high level, fuel is necessary. Desire is that fuel. It feeds the fire of success.

Delight thyself also in the Lord; and he shall give thee the desires of thine heart. Commiteth thy way unto the Lord; trust also in him; and he shall bring it to pass.

—Psalms 37:4,5

When it comes to desire, ensure you're it's master. The desire needs to be consuming, but don't let it consume you.

I'd rather have a player with 50% ability and 100% desire because the guy with 100% desire you know is going to play every day so you can make the system to fit into what he can do. The other guy—the guy with the 100% ability and 50% desire—can screw up your whole system because one day he'll be out there waltzing around.

—Coach Lombardi

Little Baby Steps to Success

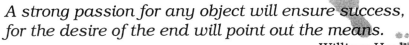

You don't succeed by mistake. You must desire it first. Desire feeds the fire of success.

A strong passion for any object will ensure success, for the desire of the end will point out the means.
—William Hazlitt

To realize, you must visualize. Visualization allows you to target success.

The difference between a successful person and others is not a lack of strength, not a lack of knowledge, but rather a lack of vision.

—Coach Lombardi

Little Baby Steps to Success

**Visualize the person you wish to become.
It will ease your path to success.**

*I don't think any team went into its game each Sunday
as well prepared as we were. We (Green Bay Packers)
knew just what to expect and we knew just how to
cope with it.*

—Paul Hornung,
Hall of Fame Halfback, Green Bay Packers

All high performers visualize before competition. Successful people from all fields visualize. So can you. Visualize to realize.

I just want to do God's will. And He's allowed me to go up to the mountain. And I've looked over and I've seen the Promised Land.

—Martin Luther King, Jr.

Many people say attitude influences altitude. They may be understating the case. Attitude defines altitude. Not successful? Check your attitude.

Nothing can stop the man with the right mental attitude from achieving his goal; nothing on earth can help the man with the wrong mental attitude.
— Thomas Jefferson

Attitude may not be subject to reason. But it is subject to action. To change your attitude, change your actions.

It is essential to understand that battles are primarily won in the hearts of men.

—Coach Lombardi

Little Baby Steps to Success

A positive attitude is a prerequisite to success. It can also be learned. Study positive thoughts daily to create a positive attitude.

It's hard to separate the mental and the physical. So much of what you do physically happens because you've thought about it and mentally prepared for it.
—Dan Fouts,
Quarterback, San Diego Chargers

Scott Fitzgerald said it was "a willingness of the heart" that made America great. Want to be great? Develop an attitude of optimism today.

Heart power is the strength of your company. Heart power is the strength of the Green Bay Packers. Heart power is the strength of America.
—Coach Lombardi

All failure is learned helplessness. All success is learned as well. To succeed, look on the positive. Begin today.

Teams don't just beat themselves. They psyche themselves out. They don't think they can win, so they don't. They get beat by doubt.

—Harry Carson,
Linebacker N. Y. Giants

Unsuccessful people say, "Why does this always happen to me?" Successful ones say, "How can I 'happen' to this?"

Success comes in cans, not in cannots.

—John Ralston

Little Baby Steps to Success

Continuous improvement does not have perfection as its goal. It has function as its goal. Develop the attitude of continuous improvement.

"Winning the first time is a lot easier than repeating as champions. To succeed again requires dedication, perseverance and, above all, discipline and mental toughness."

—Coach Lombardi

In Japan the attitude is called *kaizan*. Life is seen as a process of continuous improvement. Kaizan.

Nobody ever mastered any skill except through intensive, persistent, and intelligent practice. Practice it the right way.

—Norman Vincent Peale

There is always a better way. It's the attitude of continuous improvement.

The Wright brothers flew right through the smoke screen of impossibility.

—Charles F. Kettering

Failure is not a lack of achieving, but learning. Enjoy learning. It's a vital baby step on the way to success.

The only people who achieve much are those who want knowledge so badly that they seek it while the conditions are still unfavorable. Favorable conditions never come.

—C.S. Lewis

Learning is everywhere. Learn constantly. You'll be more successful.

Make every effort to add to your faith, goodness; and to goodness, knowledge; and to knowledge, self-control; and to self-control, perseverance; . . . for if you possess these qualities in increasing measure, they will keep you from being ineffective and unproductive.

—2 Peter 1:5-8 NIV

When you stop learning, you stop the journey to success. Don't make that mistake. Learn for a lifetime of success.

We are never going to create a good society, much less a great one, until individual excellence is once more respected and encouraged.

—Coach Lombardi

Those who run from adversity never have the opportunity to succeed. Don't deny yourself the opportunity to learn from adversity.

You never win a game unless you beat the guy in front of you. The score on the board doesn't mean a thing. That's for the fans. You've got to win the war with the man in front of you. You've got to get your man.

—Coach Lombardi

Suffering is not the enemy of success. Avoiding it is the problem. Suffering is there to make you stronger. Learn from it and you'll succeed.

There are no secrets to success. It is the result of preparation, hard work, and learning from failure.
—Colin Powell

Schedule your pain. Face the difficult challenge. All adversity results in health, but only if you face it.

In great attempts, it is glorious even to fail.
—Coach Lombardi

Does failure exist? Yes. It's in quitting. Otherwise it's a learning experience.

Show me a person who has never made a mistake and I'll show you somebody who has never achieved much.

—Joan Collins

Swing the bat. You may hit a home run. You'll never hit a home run if you don't swing the bat.

Never let the fear of striking out get in your way.
—Babe Ruth

Little Baby Steps to Success

Each time you "fail" think of what you learned. You now know one more way not to succeed. You're one baby step closer to success.

You never lose. But sometimes the clock runs out on you.

—Coach Lombardi

All success comes down to this simple formula. Those who succeed persevere. Those who don't give up too soon.

Pursue righteousness, godliness, faith, love, endurance and gentleness. Fight the good fight of faith. Take hold of eternal life to which you were called.

—1 Timothy 6:11 NIV

There is one defining characteristic that all high achievers have. They persevere long after others have given up.

Great works are performed not by strength but by perseverance.

—Samuel Johnson

Those who succeed in the long run were often the only ones still around to take advantage of the success opportunity. They persevered.

This is not easy, this effort, day after day, week after week, to keep them up, but it is essential.
— Coach Lombardi

Little Baby Steps to Success

All people face difficulty. The person with the strongest will actually sees it through. Will doesn't expend energy. It creates it.

The new leadership is in sacrifice, is in self-denial. It is in love, it is in fearlessness. It is in humility and it is in perfectly disciplined will.

—Coach Lombardi

The will to live has overcome many a terminal illness. Accept the diagnosis, not the prognosis. Develop a strong will and you will be successful.

Leadership rests not only upon ability, not only upon capacity; having the capacity to lead is not enough. The leader must be willing to use it. His leadership is then based on truth and character. There must be truth in the purpose and willpower in the character.

—Coach Lombardi

Will can keep you on path. You may stray from your goals occasionally. Strength of will brings you back in line.

Resolve to perform what you ought. Perform without fail what you resolve.

—Benjamin Franklin

Coach Lombardi said, "Love is the basis of all motivation." It's concern for your companions, family, and your success. It's caring.

Teach me to feel another's woe, To hide the fault I see; That mercy I to others show, That mercy show to me.

—Alexander Pope,
"The Universal Prayer"

Apathy is the enemy of success. You'll only succeed if you care. Dare to care.

Everybody can like somebody's strengths and somebody's good looks. But can you like somebody's weaknesses? Can you accept him for his inabilities? That's what we have to do. That's what love is. It's not just the good things.

—Coach Lombardi,
quoted by Bob Skoronski

Little Baby Steps to Success

There are no cynics on the journey to success. They give up in disbelief long before they reach their goals.

A cynic is not merely one who reads bitters lessons from the past; he is one who is prematurely disappointed in the future.

—Sydney J. Harris

Grandfather used to tell me to find something I loved and then to do it. He said to do so would result in success. I think he was right.

Where there is great love there are always miracles.
—Willa Cather

You can only succeed at those things you feel passionate about. Passion fuels success over the long course of life.

The important thought is that the Packers thrived on tough competition. We welcomed it; the team had always welcomed it. The adrenaline flowed a little quicker when we were playing tougher teams.

—Coach Lombardi

Success is not found in appearances. It's found in the doing. Passion can fuel the action necessary for long term success.

As fire consumes the forest or a flame sets the mountains ablaze, so pursue them with your tempest and terrify them with your storm.
—Psalm 83:14,15 NIV

Little Baby Steps to Success

Motivation comes from the Latin word *motus* which means "movement." Motion controls emotion. To feel motivated—move.

He (Coach Lombardi) was a master at handling and inspiring us. He's the kind of man you just have to win for.

—Paul Hornung,
Hall of Fame Halfback, Green Bay Packers

Little Baby Steps to Success

True motivation is not like a pep rally. It's in staying highly enthusiastic after the rally is over.

I've never been a losing coach, and I don't intend to start here . . . I'm going to find thirty-six men who have the pride to make any sacrifice to win. There are such men. If they're not here, I'll get them. If you are not one, if you don't want to play, you might as well leave right now.

—Coach Lombardi

If you're lacking motivation, develop a deep respect for what you're doing. Motivation arises from caring about what you do.

It takes great passion and great energy to do anything creative . . . You have to care so much that you can't sleep, you can't eat, you can't talk to people. It's just got to be right. You can't do it without that passion.

—Agnes De Mille

Little Baby Steps to Success

The response you get is the message you send. If you don't like the response, change your messages. It's totally up to you.

I am inclined to believe that a man may be free to do anything he pleases if only he will accept responsibility for whatever he does.

—Ellen Glasgow

Taking responsibility empowers you. Blaming empowers others, or the past. Empower yourself. Take responsibility.

Much is required from those to whom much is given, for their responsibility is greater.

—Luke 12:48b LB

There is one definite way to fail. Refuse to take responsibility for your behavior. The only result can be failure.

Winning is not a sometime thing; it's an all the time thing. You don't win once in awhile; you don't do the right thing once in awhile; you do them right all the time. Winning is a habit. Unfortunately, so is losing.
—Coach Lombardi

Little Baby Steps to Success

You are not your past. Don't blame it. Learn from it. You'll become more effective on your journey to success.

The past is our definition. We may strive, with good reason, to escape it, or to escape what is bad in it, but we will escape it only by adding something better to it.
—Wendell Berry

The past does not necessarily equal the present. The present does not equal the future. You only have now.

He (Coach Lombardi) made you feel like a million bucks right after you felt like two cents a minute before.

—Joe Blair

Learn from the past. Live in the present. Look to the future. It's the only formula that makes sense.

I just lump everything in a great heap labeled "the past," and, having thus emptied this deep reservoir that was once myself, I am ready to continue.

—Zelda Fitzgerald

Creative thought is the embryo of genius. Before any great work is put on paper, it was an idea in someone's mind. Creativity. It's the birth of progress.

In all my years of coaching, I have never been successful using somebody else's play . . . It makes you feel that you are losing whatever creativity you have had.

—Coach Lombardi

Create your own success. Just as you are unique, so will your success be unique. Learn from others and then create your own success.

Make visible what, without you, might perhaps never have been seen.

—Robert Bresson

Successful people are functionally creative. They rarely receive grants from the National Endowment for the Arts. For successful people, function and form go together.

Whatever creativity is, it is in part a solution to a problem.

—Brian Aldiss

Innovation combines function and creativity. It takes an idea and makes something useful from it. Innovate on the road to success. It will expedite your journey.

He (Coach Lombardi) was an innovator, willing to experiment to make his team more effective.

—Merv Hyman,

Sports writer for Englewood Press,

home of St. Cecilia High

Don't allow your problems to control you. Face your problems and then brainstorm for a way to solve them. Innovate and succeed.

The heart of the prudent acquires knowledge, And the ear of the wise seeks knowledge.

—Proverbs 18:15

One man had leftover waffles. Another man had leftover ice cream. Together they created the ice cream cone. Innovation leads to success.

Great scientific discoveries have been made by men seeking to verify quite erroneous theories about the nature of things.

—Aldous Huxley

Hydrogen is one element. Oxygen is a totally different one. Placed together in correct proportions they become water. It's called teamwork. Try it today.

He (Coach Lombardi) told us we were going to be a team. We were going to rise and fall on our faces together.

—Sonny Jurgensen,
Hall of Fame Quarterback, Washington Redskins

The Bible says, "Two are better than one, for they have a better return for their labor." It's the power of teamwork. Enlist others in your journey to success. You'll get there more quickly.

People acting together as a group can accomplish things which no individual acting alone could ever hope to bring about.

—Franklin D. Roosevelt

Individual commitment to a group effort creates a team. It's true in sports. It's also true in life. Be a team member. It will expedite your journey to success.

The finest compliment that anyone can pay to a person is to say that he is a complete team player. To deserve this tribute, your every thought, action, and deed should be one that you are doing for the team.

—Jack Pardee,
Former Head Coach, Houston Oilers

There are no prima donnas on the journey to success. Help others get what they want and they'll help you get what you want. It was true with Coach Lombardi and the Packers. And it will be true for you as well.

One man gives freely, yet gains even more; another withholds unduly, but comes to poverty.A generous man will prosper; he who refreshes others will himself be refreshed.

—Proverbs 11:24-25 NIV

Those who succeed best, serve best. It was true with Generals Colin Powel and Norman Schwarzkopf in Desert Storm. It's true with any success.

Football is a great deal like life in that it teaches that work, sacrifice, perseverance, competitive drive, selflessness and respect for authority is the price that each and every one of us must pay to achieve any goal that is worthwhile.

—Coach Lombardi

Little Baby Steps to Success

Lose yourself in the service of a greater cause. It's the quickest path to lasting success.

To serve is beautiful, but only if it is done with joy and a whole heart and free mind.

—Pearl S. Buck

Many people have said success leaves clues. They're right. Model others who have succeeded. Your success will come much more quickly.

. . . . He (Coach Lombardi) was never satisfied simply by victory. He always wanted us to play as well as we were capable of playing.

—Bart Starr,
Hall of Fame Quarterback, Green Bay Packers

There is a model for success. It's in this book. It's also in many other books. It's simple. But it's not easy. Follow the model. You will succeed.

There is a transcendent power in example. We reform others unconsciously, when we walk uprightly.
—Ann Sophie Swetchine

Little Baby Steps to Success

Study successful people. Model what they do. Repeat their paths. You will succeed beyond your wildest dreams.

Leadership is based on . . . the power to inspire others to follow.

—Coach Lombardi

All successful athletes have coaches. Michael Jordan does. Troy Aikman does. Tiger Woods does as well. Every athlete in every sport has a coach. Perhaps you could use one too.

A leader must believe in teamwork through participation. He can never close the gap between himself and the group. He must walk, as it were, a tight rope between the consent he must win and the control he must exert.

—Coach Lombardi

When Tiger Woods has a problem, he flies in his coach. They go back to basics. Practice the swing. It works for Tiger. It will work for you.

I have taught thee in the way of wisdom; I have led thee in the right paths.

—Proverbs 4:11

Michael Jordan could beat his coach in a game of one-on-one. He still has a coach. Want to be successful? Get a coach.

Coach (Lombardi) was very methodical in his approach—almost to the extent that it was boring. However, we knew what to do, when to do it and why we did it.

—John Symank,
Defensive Back, Green Bay Packers

Control is not a dirty word. Forget about others. Focus on controlling yourself. It's the only thing you have control over.

We control by attitudes—positive mental attitudes—not by rules.

—Wendy Hayes

The traffic can't control you unless you allow it. The weather and other people are powerless without your cooperation. Focus on yourself. It's the only control you have.

You had to stand up and do what was demanded of you. If it was windy, he (Coach Lombardi) wouldn't accept the wind as an excuse or if the ground were frozen you weren't allowed to slip. You had to adjust.

—Zeke Bratkowski,
Quaterback, Philadephia Eagles

Control yourself. Success requires enormous self-control. Don't worry about others. Control yourself.

He who is slow to anger is better than the mighty,
And he who rules his spirit than he who takes a city.
—Proverbs 16:32b

A leader is always ahead of the pack. They work the hardest and take the greatest risk. To be a leader, get out front. It's the only way you can be followed.

Men respond to leadership in a most remarkable way and once you have won his heart, he will follow you anywhere.

—Coach Lombardi

All leaders have a clearly defined vision. Their vision inspires. Develop a clear vision. It's necessary for the journey to success.

Leadership is the ability to get men to do what they don't want to do and like doing it.

—Harry Truman

Leaders are not necessarily eloquent speakers. But they can communicate their vision to others. Know your vision. Then communicate it.

Leadership rests not only upon ability, not only upon capacity; having the capacity to lead is not enough. The leader must be willing to use it. His leadership is then based on truth and character. There must be truth in the purpose and willpower in the character.

—Coach Lombardi

A well-defined sense of humor can help on your journey to success. It balances things out and gives you perspective. Laugh often and you'll succeed often.

We are the only creatures that both laugh and weep. I think it's because we are the only creatures that see the difference between the way things are and the way they ought to be.

—Robert Fulghum

Laughter is a natural anti-depressant. It helps regulate mood, improves cardiovascular endurance, and increases immunity. Laugh, live, and learn. It's a true formula for success.

A merry heart maketh a cheerful countenance.
—Proverbs 15:13a

Laugh at yourself. Take your work seriously, but not yourself. It will help you on the journey to success.

You grow up when you have your first real laugh.
—Ethel Barrymore

Balance. It's a holy word. Successful people develop balance in their lives. It equals out the stress of success and allows you to peak over the long term.

I think good physical conditioning is essential to any occupation. A man who is physically fit performs better at any job. Fatigue makes cowards of us all.
—Coach Lombardi

On the journey to success balance is vital. Too much work will burn you out. Too much rest, and you'll never succeed. Find balance in your life.

Work, alternated with needful rest, is the salvation of man or woman.

—Antoinette Brown Blackwell

Schedule the important things in your life to maintain balance. There is a recipe that will work for you. It's unique to you. Find it and balance your life.

Work is not the curse, but drudgery is.
—Henry Ward Beecher

We all need feedback. Sometimes the feedback is positive. Occasionally it can be outright harsh. But it's all necessary for success.

Do not let any unwholesome talk come out of your mouths, but only what is helpful for building others up according to their needs, that it may benefit those who listen.

—Ephesians 4:29 NIV

Most people who give feedback have good intentions. Others want to hurt you. Realize it for what it is. Accept what you can. Ignore the rest.

All my life I've done things others said couldn't be done.

—Ted Turner

When people try to hurt you, don't waste time getting even. Get successful instead.

When everyone said that I'd never be any good again, it just made me push on.

—Evonne Goolagong

Little Baby Steps to Success

When the horse is dead—dismount.

It takes a special kind of character to know when to let up, and when to back off.

—Tom Landry,
Talking about Coach Lombardi

Little Baby Steps to Success

If something isn't working, fix it. If you can't, consider changing course. Your destination is success. There's more than one way to get there.

There are two ways of meeting difficulties. You alter the difficulties or you alter yourself to meet them.
—Phyliss Bottome

Good pilots never go through a thunder-storm. Around, underneath, or above. But never through. There is more than one way to reach a destination.

We must dare and dare again and keep on daring.
—George Danton

Faith is not easy. Cynicism is. Yet faith is necessary for success. Practice it daily. It will help you achieve your dreams.

According to your faith be it unto you.

—Matthew 9:29b

Successful people have faith in a higher power. Faith builds their self-confidence and optimism. Believe in yourself. But also believe in something greater than yourself.

I pray hard, work hard and leave the rest to God.
—Florence Griffith Joyner

Little Baby Steps to Success

Faith can lead to more success. Continuous success will lead to greater faith. Try it. It will speed you on your journey to success.

A man who is trained to his peak capacity will gain confidence. Confidence is contagious and so is lack of confidence.

—Coach Lombardi

Successful people are usually deeply spiritual. They have a profound relationship with God. Investigate this on your own. It will expedite your journey to success.

If we prepare thoughtfully, work hard, have faith in God's plan for us and are honest with ourselves, we can most closely reach the perfection of our talents.
—Stan Smith

Coach Lombardi was deeply spiritual. He had a deep abiding faith. He credited much of his success to this relationship. It can have an impact on you too.

Now faith is the substance of things hoped for, the evidence of things not seen.

—Hebrews 11:1

Spirituality is not a shallow concept. It's far deeper than most people can imagine. Develop your spirituality at a deep level. It will aid your journey to success

The greatest secret for eliminating the inferiority complex, which is another term for deep and profound self-doubt, is to fill your mind to overflowing with faith.

—Norman Vincent Peale

Little Baby Steps to Success

You can succeed. It's simple. But not easy. Follow the blueprint in this book. If you do you'll succeed. Add courage. And you'll remain successful.

There's only one way to succeed in anything, and that is to give everything.

—Coach Lombardi

Books by Starburst Publishers

(Partial listing—full list available on request)

"Little" Baby Steps to Success —Vince Lombardi Jr. & John Q. Baucom

Subtitled: *52 Vince Lombardi-Inspired Ways to Make Your Life Successful.*
Motivational, inspiring and filled with insight that will get you off the bench and
into the game of success. This wisdom-filled, pocket-sized collection of the best of
Lombardi will help you one small step at a time to reach the goals you have
imagined.

(trade paper) ISBN: 0914984969 **$6.95**

Baby Steps to Success —Vince Lombardi Jr. & John Q. Baucom

Subtitled: *Vince Lombardi-Inspired Motivational Wisdom & Insight to Make Your
Life Successful.* Vince Lombardi's is one of the most quoted success stories in the
history of the world. From corporate boardrooms to athletic locker rooms, his
wisdom is studied, read, and posted on walls. The same skills that Coach
Lombardi used to turn the Green Bay Packers from cellar dwellers to world
champions is now available to you in *Baby Steps To Success.* This book can help
you be more successful in your career, personal or family life. The same principles
that made the Packers Super Bowl champions can make you a "Super Bowl"
employee, parent or spouse. These principles are broken down into 52 unique and
achievable "Baby Steps."

(trade paper) ISBN: 0914984950 **$12.95**

"Little" Baby Steps to Happiness —John Q. Baucom

Subtitled: *Inspiring Quotes and Affirmations to Make Your Life Happy.* This portable collection of quotes and affirmations from *Baby Steps to Happiness* will encourage Happiness one "little" footstep at a time. This book is the perfect personal "cheerleader."

(trade paper) ISBN 091498487X **$6.95**

Baby Steps to Happiness —John Q. Baucom

Subtitled: *52 Inspiring Ways to Make Your Life Happy.* This unique 52-step approach will enable the reader to focus on small steps that bring practical and proven change. The author encourages the reader to take responsibility for the happiness that only he can find. Chapter titles, such as, *Have a Reason to Get Out of Bed, Deal with Your Feelings or Become Them, Would You Rather Be Right or Happy?*, and *Love To Win More Than You Hate to Lose* give insight and encouragement on the road to happiness.

(trade paper) ISBN 0914984861 **$12.95**

Purchasing Information: Books are available from your favorite Bookstore, either from current stock or special order. To assist bookstore in locating your selection be sure to give title, author, and ISBN #. If unable to purchase from the bookstore you may order direct from STARBURST PUBLISHERS. When ordering enclose full payment plus $3.00 for shipping and handling ($4.00 if Canada or Overseas). Payment in US Funds only. Please allow two to three weeks minimum (longer overseas) for delivery. Make checks payable to and mail to STARBURST PUBLISHERS, P.O. Box 4123, LANCASTER, PA 17604. Credit card orders may also be placed by calling 1-800-441-1456 (credit card orders only), Mon-Fri, 8 a.m. – 5 p.m. Eastern Time. **Prices subject to change without notice.** Catalog available for a 9 x 12 self-addressed envelope with 4 first-class stamps. 09-97